AnimArt Publishing

CAT MANDALAS

Coloring Book for Cat Lovers

Amazing book to enhance your artistic mind
and provide hours of relaxation

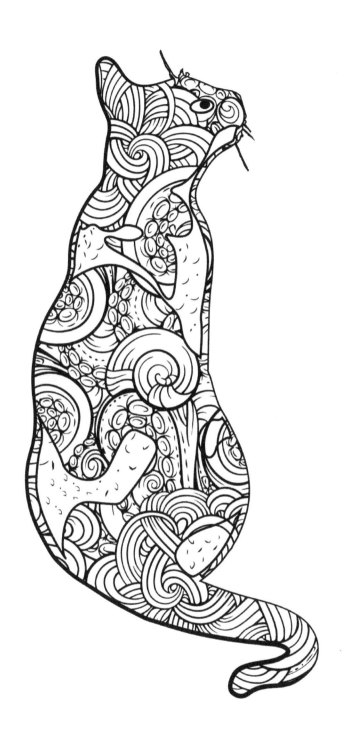

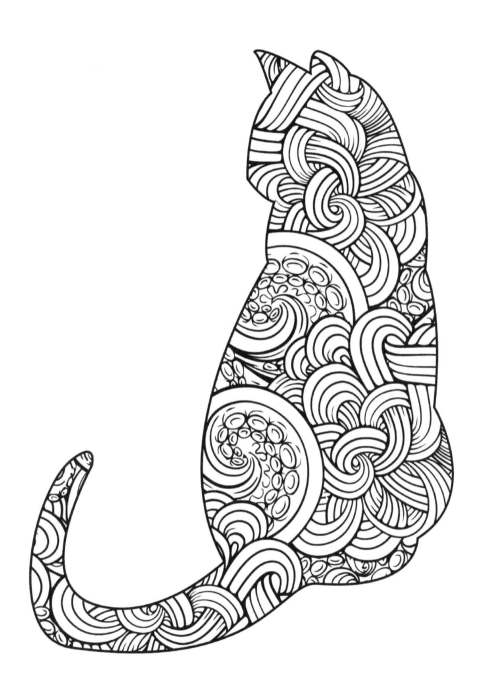

CPSIA information can be obtained
at www.ICGtesting.com
Printed in the USA
BVHW021055300323
661447BV00009B/543